Science

Library of Congress Cataloging in Publication Data

Allington, Richard L.
  Science.

  (Beginning to learn about)
  Summary: Text and suggested activities introduce
the scientific method, an orderly procedure for
discoveries and for solving problems.
    1. Science—Juvenile literature.   [1. Science—
Methodology]   I. Krull, Kathleen.   II. Teason,
James G., ill.   III. Title.   IV. Series.
Q163.A435   1982   502'.8   82-10171
ISBN 0-8172-1387-2

Library of Congress Number: 82-10171

  2 3 4 5 6 7 8 9 0 86 85 84

Printed in the United States of America.

Richard L. Allington is Associate Professor, Department of Reading,
State University of New York at Albany.
Kathleen Krull is the author of twenty-nine books for children.

BEGINNING TO LEARN ABOUT

SCIENCE

BY RICHARD L. ALLINGTON, PH.D., · AND KATHLEEN KRULL

ILLUSTRATED BY JAMES TEASON

Raintree Childrens Books · Milwaukee · Toronto · Mexico City · London

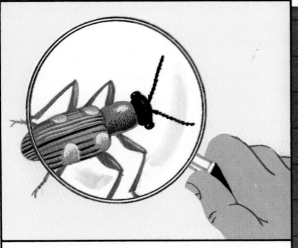

looking closely at things

asking questions

measuring and comparing

research

How do we find out about
the world we live in?
We find things out through **science**.

sorting things out

testing and experimenting

exploring

keeping records

This book will show you ways to find out things about yourself and your world.

Look closely at this picture.
Write down or tell someone
everything you see.

Ask your friends to tell you
what they see. Did they see
anything you missed?

Now look closely at this picture.
Pretend you *are* something in
this picture—an animal, a plant,
or a thing.

What are you pretending to be?
Write down or tell someone about
what it's like to be that thing.
What would your day be like?

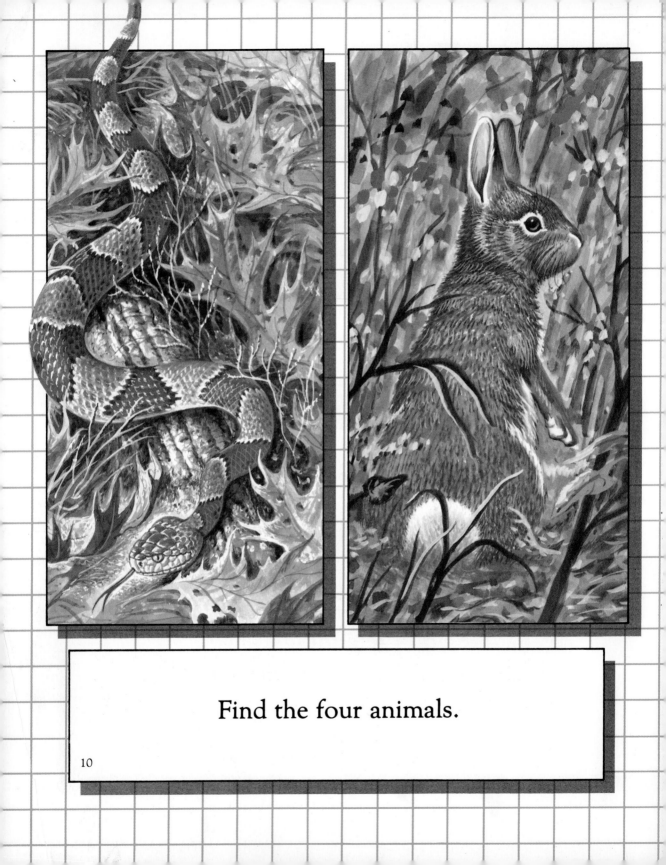

Find the four animals.

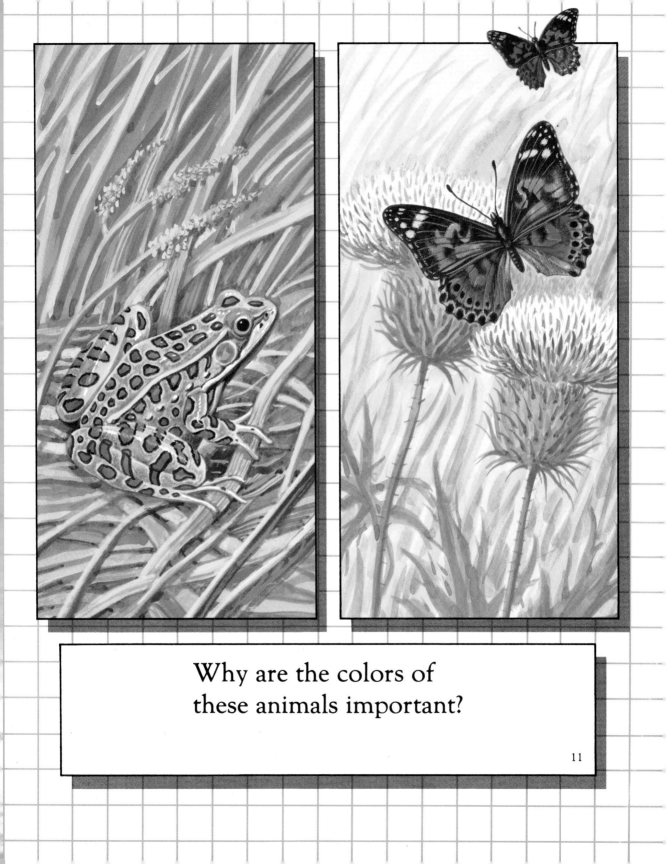

Why are the colors of
these animals important?

Look at this picture.
Find things that are getting bigger.

Now draw a picture of *your*
neighborhood. Put in something
that is getting bigger.

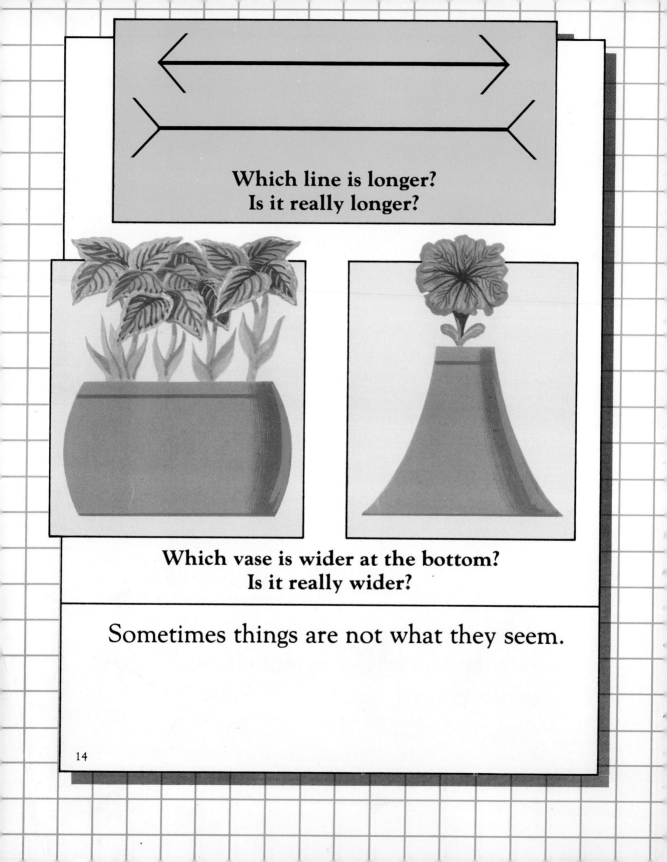

Which line is longer?
Is it really longer?

Which vase is wider at the bottom?
Is it really wider?

Sometimes things are not what they seem.

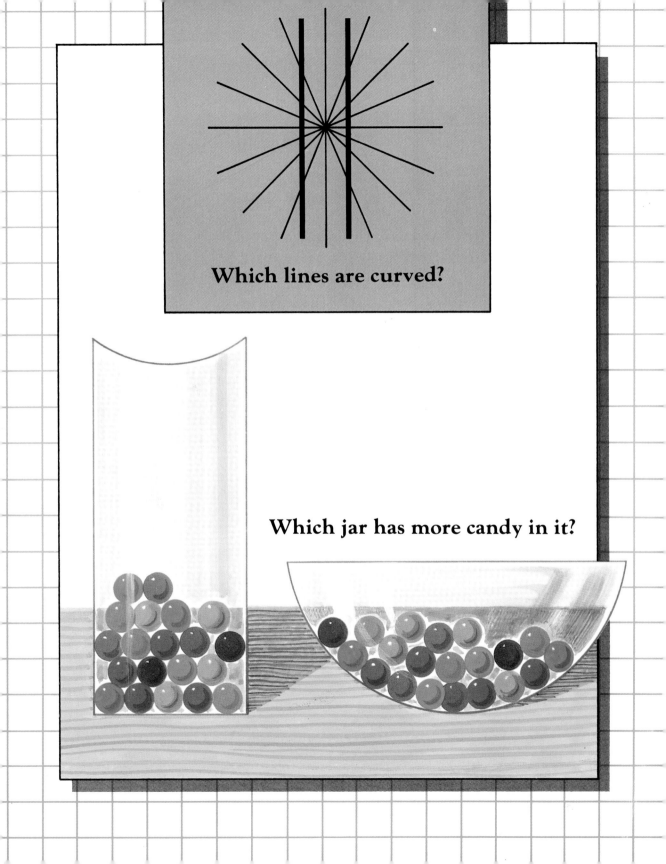

Which lines are curved?

Which jar has more candy in it?

You can look at things even more closely with a magnifying glass. Find five things around your house to look at with a magnifying glass.

Write down or tell someone how
each thing looks different when you
use the magnifying glass.

Look closely at this picture.
What shapes or patterns do
you see in the stars?

Pick a clear night and look
at the sky. Draw a picture
of what you see.

	color of the sky in the morning	color of the sky in the afternoon	shape of the moon
Sunday			
Monday			🌙
Tuesday			🌙
Wednesday			🌙
Thursday			🌙
Friday			🌙
Saturday			🌕

You can find out about weather by
looking, measuring, and keeping records.

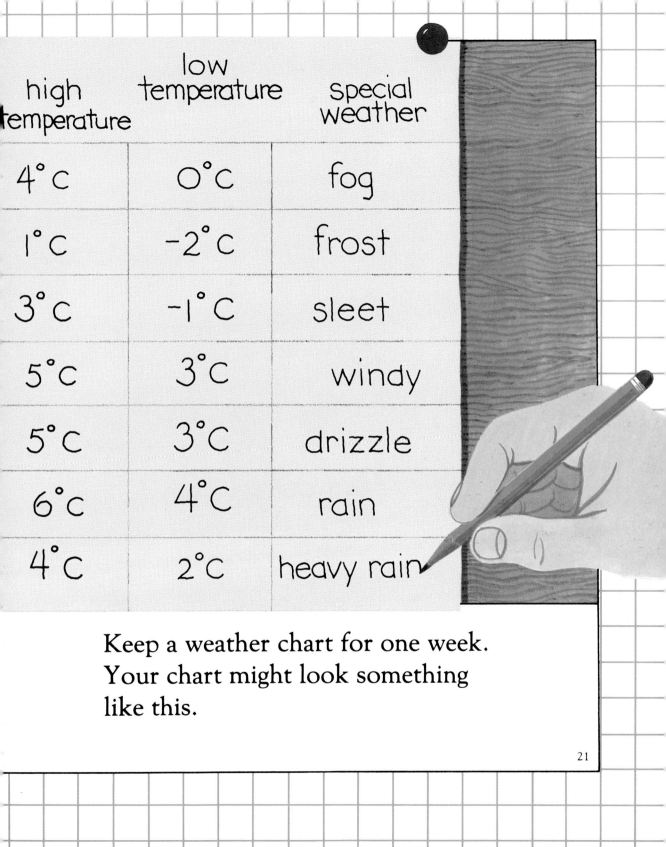

high temperature	low temperature	special weather
4°c	0°c	fog
1°c	-2°c	frost
3°c	-1°C	sleet
5°c	3°c	windy
5°c	3°c	drizzle
6°c	4°c	rain
4°c	2°c	heavy rain

Keep a weather chart for one week.
Your chart might look something
like this.

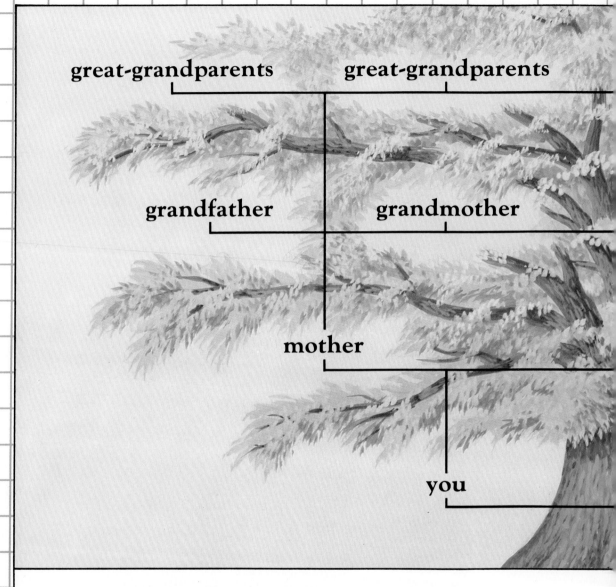

great-grandparents great-grandparents

grandfather grandmother

mother

you

Another kind of chart is a family tree. Ask someone in your family to help you make a family tree. Write down the name of each person.

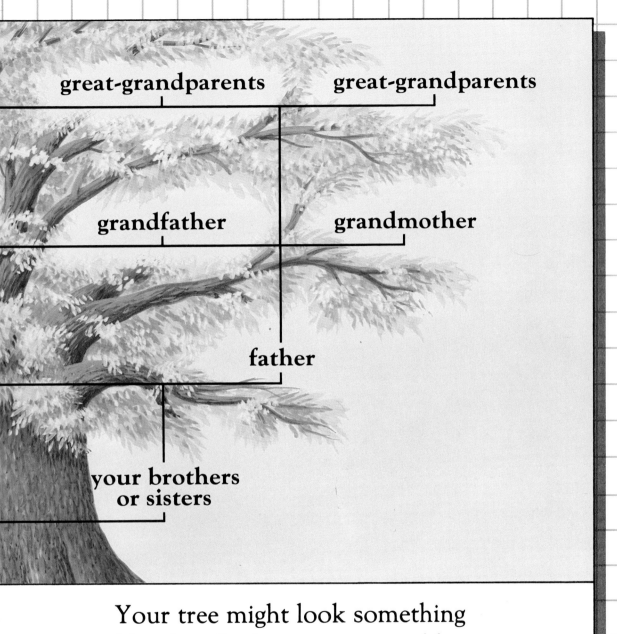

great-grandparents   great-grandparents

grandfather   grandmother

father

your brothers
or sisters

Your tree might look something
like this. Perhaps you can add
even more names.

In your family, who has the biggest
hands? On a piece of paper, trace
a picture of one of your hands.
Measure each finger.

24

Now trace the hands of people in your family. Who has the biggest hands?

Make a poster that shows how you are
unique—different from your family and
friends. You can use photographs, pictures
or words from magazines or newspapers,
your own drawings, or real things.

Tape or paste everything onto a
large piece of paper. Perhaps this
poster will give you some ideas.

Plant several bean seeds in each of
two pots. Keep the dirt wet until
after the seeds have sprouted. Then
put one pot in a sunny window.

Keep the other pot away from the window. Keep a record of what happens to each plant. Which plant grows taller? Why?

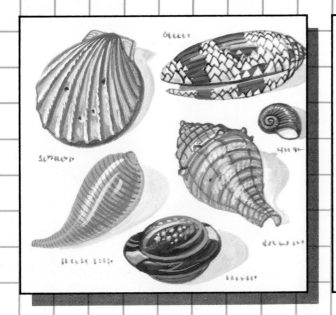

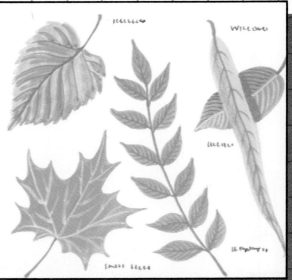

What kinds of things do you like
to collect? If possible, take
your collection to school.

Talk about how you sort your collection. Talk about how you find things for your collection.

Make your own book about science.
Look through newspapers and magazines.
Try to find pictures of people doing
the things that are mentioned on
pages 4 and 5 of this book.
Cut out the pictures.
Tape or paste them onto pieces of paper.
Fasten the papers together.
Talk about your book
to your family or friends.
Say what each person is trying find out.
You may ask an adult to help you.

Make a list of five things you
would like to know more about.
How do you think you
would start finding out
about each thing?